Study Guide for
Dracula

—by Bram Stoker—

Edited by
Eleanor Bourg Nicholson

Series Editor
Joseph Pearce

Introduction by
Patrick S. J. Carmack

IGNATIUS PRESS   SAN FRANCISCO

Cover design by John Herreid

© 2012 Ignatius Press, San Francisco
All rights reserved

ISBN 978-1-58617-497-2

Printed in India ⊗

Table of Contents

Why a Great Books Study Guide?

Wisdom is generally acknowledged to be the highest good of the human mind, whether this be recognized as knowledge of first principles and causes or as a contemplative gaze at Wisdom itself. But how does one obtain wisdom? The means is primarily conversation with great and wise persons who have already advanced far along the paths of knowledge and understanding to wisdom. As the philosopher Dr. Peter Redpath succinctly puts it when addressing audiences of young people interested in understanding why they ought to read great books, "If you wish to become wise, learn from wise people."

Since, however, persons of great wisdom are rare and generally unavailable to us due to distance or death, we enter into conversation with them through their books which record their thought. In doing this, we soon discover how all the authors of great books used this same method of study themselves. They began by conversing with or reading the great books written by the sages of earlier generations. In so doing, they avoided having to re-invent the wheel each generation; and they avoided making mistakes already dealt with and were able to build on existing foundations. Indeed what would be the point in studying mediocre works by lesser luminaries or beginning all thought over from square one every few years, when great books by the wisest people—the great sages of civilization—are readily available?

> The reading of all good books is indeed like a conversation with the noblest men of past centuries who were the authors of them, nay a carefully studied conversation, in which they reveal to us none but the best of their thoughts. (Rene Descartes, *Discourse on Method*)

5

Through the internal dialectical process found in the great books—the references, discussions, critiques, and responses to the thought of the authors' wise predecessors, a process referred to as the "Great Conversation" by Robert M. Hutchins—we may closely follow the development of the investigations conducted by these wise men into the great ideas they have pondered and about which they have written. This manner of study has always been the normative approach to wisdom in the West.

> Until lately the West has regarded it as self-evident that the road to education lay through great books. No man was educated until he was acquainted with the masterpieces of his tradition. . . . They were the principal instruments of liberal education. . . . The goal toward which Western society moves is the Civilization of the Dialogue. The spirit of Western civilization is the spirit of inquiry. Its dominant element is *Logos*.[1]

No ongoing dialogue comparable in duration or breadth exists in the East. Pope Benedict XVI has mentioned that Western civilization has become the dominant civilization because of its closer correspondence to human nature. In his 2006 Regensburg lecture, he noted that there exists a real analogy between our created reason and God, who is *Logos* (meaning both "reason" and "word"). To abandon reason—and hence the dialogue, which is both reason's natural expression and necessary aid—would be contrary both to the nature of man and of God. This cumulative wisdom of the West is preserved and transmitted in its great music and art, but most particularly in the study of its great books which record the results of three millennia of dialogue, guided by reason, concerning the most profound ideas with which we must all grapple such as existence, life, love, happiness, and so forth.

---

[1] Robert M. Hutchins, *The Great Conversation: The Substance of a Liberal Education*, vol. 1, *The Great Books of the Western World* (Chicago: Encyclopedia Britannica, Inc., 1952).

This manner of learning is greatly facilitated when the reader also engages in a dialectic exchange—a live conversation (in person or now online)—with other readers of the same books, probing and discussing the great ideas contained in them and, one hopes, carrying them a few steps further. This method of learning is often referred to as the Socratic method, after the ancient Athenian philosopher Socrates, who initiated its use as a deliberate way to obtain understanding and wisdom through mutual inquiry and discussion. This same "questioning" method was used by Christ, who often answered questions with other questions, parables, and stories that left the hearers wondering, questioning, and thinking. He already knew the answers, as Socrates often did. The goal was not merely indoctrination of the memory with information, facts, and knowledge, but mind- and life-changing understanding and wisdom.

This study guide is intended for students (if one is still learning, one is a student) who have read—extensively—lesser works, particularly the classic children's literature. Given that degree of preparation, students of high school age and older, including adults, can pick up Homer's *Iliad* and *Odyssey* or Herodotus' *Histories* and other great works and enter into the seminal thought of the most influential books of our culture and civilization. There is reason not to delay such education.

The great books are, for the most part, the most interesting and well written of all books. They were not written for experts. Their wide and enduring appeal to generation after generation testifies to that fact. Readers reasonably prepared for them will find them captivating, entertaining, and enlightening. Naturally, some readers will profit more than others from the great books, but all will profit from learning about the Trojan War, ancient civilizations, the heroes of ancient Greece, the early tragedies, and the thought of Aristotle. Works such as Genesis, the *Aeneid*, Saint Augustine's *Confessions*, Chaucer's *Canterbury Tales*, Dante's *Divine Comedy*, Saint Thomas Aquinas' *Summa theologica*, and Shakespeare's plays are foundational for and/or profoundly influential on our way of life. These works are essential for participation in the Great Conversation mentioned above. The enduring intellectual dialogue begins with the works of Homer, the "father of civilization", and proceeds through the centuries, eventually absorbing the Old and New Testaments in a lengthy reformulation of classical civilization into Western civilization, which continues—albeit always under assault by various errors—right up to our time.

The principal guides in selecting the works of enduring appeal to be included in the corpus of great books, besides generations of readers, include the late, great Dr. Mortimer J. Adler, who worked for eighty years (from 1921 to 2000, when I had the privilege to participate in his last Socratic discussion groups) to restore and keep the great classics, including particularly those by Plato, Aristotle, and Aquinas, in the Western canon of great books. As Dr. Adler put it, "The great books constitute the backbone of a liberal education." But read alone in our postmodernist context of radical skepticism, the great books can easily be misunderstood and used for all manner of mischief. It was precisely a desire to provide a deeper understanding of the importance and influence of the great books—to highlight what is true and great in them and to expose and defang what is false—that inspired Ignatius Press to initiate its important Critical Editions series.

Augmenting the work of Dr. Adler, on behalf of Ignatius Press, is Joseph Pearce, the author of several critically acclaimed, bestselling biographies of great authors, who has diligently worked as the author and/or editor of these study guides to accompany the Ignatius Critical Editions, of which he is also the series editor. Our gratitude extends to Father Joseph Fessio for his encouragement of this much-needed project, which is so broad in scope and vision as to be potentially revolutionary in the schools, colleges, and universities dominated by relativism. Homeschoolers, though somewhat shielded from the relativism of the schools, will find in these guides a welcome and trustworthy means of introduction to the great books and to their careful and critical reading.

Finally, it is worth emphasizing that these Ignatius Critical Editions Study Guides are merely introductory guides with tests, questions, and answer keys helpful for student assessment. The great books themselves are the primary texts, their authors our primary teachers.

Patrick S. J. Carmack
January 18, 2008

Patrick S. J. Carmack, J.D., is the president of the Great Books Academy Homeschool Program (greatbooksacademy.org), the Angelicum Academy Homeschool Program (angelicum.net), the Western Civilization Foundation, and the online publication *Classical Homeschooling Magazine* (classicalhomeschooling.com).

How to Use This Guide

The Ignatius Critical Editions (ICE) Study Guides are intended to assist students and teachers in their reading of the Ignatius Critical Editions. Each guide gives a short introductory appraisal of the contextual factors surrounding the writing of the literary work, a short "bare bones" summary of the plot, and a more in-depth summary of some of the essential critical aspects of the work. There is also a list of things to think about while reading the book, designed to focus the reader's critical faculties. These points to ponder will enable the reader to rise above a merely recreational reading of the text to a level of critical and literary appreciation befitting the work itself.

Finally, there are questions for the student to answer. These fall into two distinct categories: questions concerned with a knowledge of the *facts* of the work, and questions concerned with analyzing the *truths* that emerge from the work. This approach is rooted in the fundamental axiom, taught by great philosophers such as Aristotle and Saint Thomas Aquinas, that we must go *through* the facts *to* the truth. Put simply, an inadequate knowledge of the facts of a work (who did what and when, who said what to whom, etc.) will inevitably lead to a failure to understand the work on its deeper levels of meaning.

As such, readers of the work are strongly encouraged to answer all the *fact-related* questions in part 1. The close reading of the text that this will entail will prepare them for the essay questions in part 2. With regard to the latter, it is left to the discretion of the teacher (or the reader) as to how many of these questions should be answered. Some of the questions, particularly those calling for a contextual reading of the work in relation to other works, might be unsuitable for less-advanced students or readers. In such cases, the teacher (or reader) should use his discretion in deciding which of the essay questions should be answered. In any event, you have been provided with an abundance of questions from which to choose!

Teachers should also be aware that the answer key can be removed before the study guide is made available to the student. Answers to the questions in the "Bare Bones" and "Things to Think About" sections are not included in the answer key because these questions are intended to raise issues for the student to ponder and are not intended to be employed for examination purposes.

It should be noted that the Ignatius Critical Editions and the ICE Study Guides approach these great works of literature from a tradition-oriented perspective. Those seeking deconstruction, "queer theory", feminism, postcolonialism, and other manifestations of the latest academic fads and fashions will be disappointed. If you are unable to think outside the postmodern box, this guide is not for you!

Context

The origin of the English literary heritage of vampires is closely linked with that of the horror story. In 1816, while living at a villa beside Lake Geneva, Lord Byron wrote a fragment of a story that John William Polidori, his personal physician, later developed into the novella *The Vampire* (1819). It was at the same time and in this same place that the eighteen-year-old Mary Godwin (mistress of the poet Percy Bysshe Shelley and soon to be his wife) scribbled the first lines of *Frankenstein* (1818). The early association of the fledgling English vampiric tradition with Byron would prove of great significance; Polidori, in *The Vampire*, closely modeled the figure of a suave, aristocratic, charismatic, sexual predator on the notorious Romantic poet. A stream of vampiric works followed by various authors, most of them with villains in the Byronic mold. These works include the penny dreadful serial *Varney, the Vampire* (1845–1847), Sheridan Le Fanu's *Carmilla* (1872), Henri Guy de Maupassant's *La Horla* (1887), and Arthur Conan Doyle's "The Sussex Vampire" (1896, not published until 1924).

Dracula enjoys a special place among these works—an honor derived greatly from the many innovative additions its author made to the vampiric tradition. When Bram Stoker, a former Irish civil servant, began research for *Dracula*, he was the business manager of the Lyceum Theatre, home to the consummate actor Henry Irving. His intimate knowledge of the theatrical world and of the extraordinary figure of Irving introduced a dramatic flair into his work. Many even discern in the figure of Count Dracula a close resemblance to Stoker's employer and friend. As an Irishman,

Stoker was a connoisseur of eerie and darkly haunting Irish folk and fairy tales. He had penned a number of short stories and more than one quasi-Gothic novel, but nothing on the scale of *Dracula*. For his vampiric magnum opus, Stoker dedicated an extraordinary amount of time to research and writing; he spent seven years on *Dracula*, putting in long hours at the British Library and exploring the coastal town of Whitby. It was in Whitby that he discovered the name Dracula in William Wilkinson's *An Account of the Principalities of Wallachia and Moldavia*.[1] In many ways, as a consequence, *Dracula* owes more to folklore than to the Byronic legacy.

Stoker drew on many other literary traditions as well. In *Dracula*, he brought the epistolary form to its full potential, incorporating a wide assortment of documents—including letters, diary entries, newspaper clippings, telegrams, ship's logs, and memoranda—while at the same time making generous use of the scientific precision of his own period. *Dracula* also bears marked similarities to the rambunctious adventure stories that were gaining popularity toward the end of the Victorian period, including the works of Robert Louis Stevenson, Arthur Conan Doyle, Rudyard Kipling, and H. G. Wells. Their works strike a markedly different tone from the historical romance novels of Sir Walter Scott, which dominated the literary scene in the early half of the century. There is a sense of temporal urgency in these works; unlike Scott's forays into the romantic past, these adventures unfold in the present time, standing on the brink of an unknown new world as the tumultuous Victorian period came to a close.

The reign of Queen Victoria, from 1837 to 1901, was longer than that of any other English monarch. This comparative monarchical stability strikingly contrasts with the profound societal changes then occurring, the effects of many of which can be seen in *Dracula*: the Industrial Revolution, which brought spectacular urban growth

---

[1] A list of Stoker's other sources is provided in the Ignatius Critical Editions publication of the novel: Bram Stoker, *Dracula*, ed. Eleanor Bourg Nicholson, Ignatius Critical Editions (San Francisco: Ignatius Press, 2012), p. xxiii–xxiv.

as well as technological advancement; dramatic advances in natural science and medicine; changing ideas in natural philosophy; shifting undercurrents across a wide range of religious movements, exacerbated by the challenges to belief posed by scientific theories such as Darwinism; imperial advancement and political tensions at home and abroad; and much more. The threats that beset the protagonists of *Dracula*, though high fantastical in their trappings, were not unreal for the fin-de-siècle Englishman. Could society remain stable when scientific advancement seemed to threaten religious belief and when technological marvels seemed to threaten the most sacred of societal institutions: the family? In the end, could all of the advances of science and technology really support man in a battle against the supernatural?

It is precisely at this juncture of waxing scientism and waning faith that *Dracula* appears on the scene. At its core is the tension between science and the supernatural. In the light of uncertain modernity, *Dracula* remains an intriguing and bizarre metaphysical problem.

Bare Bones: The Skeleton Plot

The text of *Dracula* is a collection of journal and diary entries, letters, newspaper clippings, telegrams, and memoranda, composed by characters in the course of the novel. These collectively provide an account of an attempt by a Transylvanian count to take up residence in London.

The novel begins on May 3 as Jonathan Harker, a solicitor working for a Mr. Hawkins of Exeter, journeys from England to Transylvania on business for Count Dracula. On his way he commences a journal in shorthand. He records copious notes describing his physical and cultural surroundings. Many notes are particularly meant for Mina Murray (later introduced as his fiancée). His journal entries record details of his travel from Bistritz to the Count's castle, and the strange, superstitious behavior of the local people. He arrives at the castle near midnight on May 4, the eve of Saint George's Day—when "all the evil things in the world . . . have full sway" (see *Dracula*, p. 20). His aristocratic host welcomes him into the castle with the chilling invitation: "Welcome to my house! Enter freely and of your own will!" (see *Dracula*, p. 34).

At first fascinated, Harker soon becomes unnerved by his unusual surroundings and by the strange behavior of the mysterious Count. Dracula tells him many tales of Transylvanian history and of his own heritage. In turn Harker provides information concerning England and the house the solicitor has secured for Dracula there: the medieval Carfax estate, at Purfleet, next door to a private lunatic asylum.

One morning while he is shaving before a small mirror, Harker is surprised to be greeted by the Count (surprised because Dracula has no reflection in the mirror). Startled, Harker cuts himself with the razor. The sight of blood affects Dracula strangely. In a fury, he grabs at Harker's throat but falls back when his fingers touch a beaded string bearing a crucifix around Harker's neck. Dracula then destroys the mirror and leaves Harker alone for some time. Harker considers how odd it is that he has never seen Dracula eat or drink. For the first time, Harker glances out of a window in daylight and sees the scenery: the castle is on the edge of a precipice, "a veritable prison, and [he is] a prisoner" (see *Dracula*, p. 50).

As the days pass, Harker becomes more distrustful of Dracula and more concerned as to his own fate. The Count instructs him to write home announcing his intention of remaining at the castle for another month. Harker's adventures become increasingly alarming: witnessing the Count crawling out of a window and down the side of the castle headfirst like a lizard, and nearly being attacked by three beautiful—and shadowless—young women. With each passing day, Harker's doom seems to become more certain, especially as the Count orders him to write postdated letters indicating his travel home. When a band of Szgany (gypsies) arrives in the courtyard, Harker attempts to bribe them to send out word of his real predicament, but the gypsies intercept the letters and hand them over to Dracula.

Near the end of June, Harker escapes from his room into the forbidden rooms of the house. He discovers an old, ruined chapel that contains fifty great boxes, in one of which he finds Count Dracula lying atop a pile of earth, seeming "either dead or asleep", and in his eyes "a look of hate" that so terrifies Harker that he flees (see *Dracula*, p. 79). Over the next few days, the gypsies pack up the boxes, loading them onto wagons for shipment to London. On June 29 Dracula tells his prisoner that they will part on the following day, causing Harker to anticipate that he will soon die. He returns to the chapel on June 30 and once again finds Dracula in his box—looking strangely youthful and with blood on his lips. Harker strikes the Count on the head with a shovel, leaving a scar, then flees to his room. Later, realizing that the Szgany have nearly finished their work, Harker decides it would be better to die attempting to escape than to stay with the "awful women". He then entrusts himself to God's mercy: "At least God's mercy is better than that of these monsters, and the precipice is steep and high. At its foot a man may sleep—as a man. Good-bye, all! Mina!" (see *Dracula*, p. 85).

Meanwhile, in England, Mina Murray, an assistant schoolmistress, corresponds with her friend Lucy Westenra. Their letters (beginning on May 9) speak of Mina's practice at writing shorthand, her preparations for marriage and desire to serve her husband, and exciting developments in Lucy's love life. Lucy reports that she has received three proposals of marriage in one day: first from Dr. John Seward, who is in charge of a lunatic asylum; then from Mr. Quincey P. Morris, an adventurer from Texas; and finally from Mr. Arthur Holmwood, the only son of Lord Godalming—whose proposal she accepts.

On the day after the proposals, Seward's diary (kept in phonograph) first appears. He grieves for his loss of Lucy but focuses on his work and particularly on one patient, R. M. Renfield, a man "so unlike the normal lunatic" (see *Dracula*, p. 95). At the same time, Seward maintains his friendship with Morris and Holmwood, despite the latter's triumph over the two other men in love.

In late July, Mina commences her journal in the northern English coastal town of Whitby, where she is vacationing with Lucy and Lucy's mother. Mina provides a detailed account of her surroundings, particularly the harbor, and her conversation with Mr. Swales, a talkative old seadog. He tells her of the tombstones in the Church of Saint Mary's, at the top of the Whitby cliff, including a tombstone under the bench where she and Lucy love to sit: it is over the grave of a suicide. Meanwhile, as Lucy eagerly anticipates her upcoming marriage, Mina is "just a little heart-sick", thinking of Jonathan, from whom she has not heard for some time (see *Dracula*, pp. 106–7).

Back in London, Seward continues studying Renfield's case over the course of July. The lunatic catches flies, then spiders to whom he feeds the flies, and then is caught eating the flies himself. When Renfield captures a sparrow to which he feeds his spiders, Seward begins to see the "method in his madness" (see *Dracula*, p. 109). Within a few days, with the spiders and the flies almost all gone, Renfield asks for a kitten. Seward refuses, infuriating the patient, whom Seward now considers "an undeveloped homicidal maniac" (see *Dracula*, p. 110). Renfield eats his birds raw and returns to trapping flies. Seward then outlines his theoretical diagnosis: Renfield is a "zoöphagous (life-eating) maniac", desiring to "absorb as many lives as he can, and he has laid himself out to achieve it in a cumulative way" (see *Dracula*, p. 111).

In Whitby, Mina's journal continues with frequent updates. Now she is not only concerned for Harker but is also worried about Lucy, who speaks of strange dreams and has resumed her old habit of sleepwalking. In early August, a sudden and spectacular storm besets Whitby, introducing an eerie atmosphere into the entire town. In addition to her own observations, Mina inserts into her diary a newspaper account of the storm and of the dramatic and seemingly miraculous arrival of the Russian schooner *Demeter* in the midst of the storm. There is no one aboard except the dead body of the captain, and a dog who leaps from the boat when it lands. It carries a cargo of wooden boxes of mould addressed to a Whitby solicitor. The newspaper publishes the log of the *Demeter*, describing its terrifying passage from Varna to Whitby, and the descent of the crew and the captain into bewilderment and terror. A coroner's court brings in an open verdict, and the Whitby populace praises the captain as a hero and gives him a public funeral.

With the coming of the storm and the subsequent arrival of the schooner, Lucy becomes even more restless. Mr. Swales is discovered dead by the seat where Mina and Lucy have frequently visited him. On the night of August 10, Mina awakens in the night and finds Lucy gone. Mina runs out to find her sleepwalking friend up on the cliffs with a dark figure bending over her. When Mina arrives at the bench, Lucy is alone. Mina wraps her in a shawl and takes her home, putting her to bed.

After this "agonising experience" (see *Dracula*, p. 137), Lucy's sleepwalking and strange behavior increase. Mina sees a bat near the bedroom window more than once, and an unsettling stranger with burning eyes watching them up on the cliffs. Lucy appears increasingly anemic with neck wounds that will not heal.

In the middle of August, a Whitby solicitor corresponds briefly with a London shipping company regarding the transference of Count Dracula's boxes to Carfax. At around the same time, Lucy's health improves, and to Mina's delight, word comes of Jonathan at last. On August 12, Sister Agatha of the Hospital of Saint Joseph and Sainte Mary, Budapest, writes to inform Mina that Harker has been under the hospital's care for nearly six weeks. He appears to be suffering from a violent brain fever. The sister invites Mina to come and fetch her fiancé. In a postscript, the sister hints at dark and frightening things, cautioning Mina to be patient and gentle with him.

Even as Lucy's future looks brighter, Seward records dramatic changes in Renfield, beginning on August 19, when he lapses into a form of "religious mania" and declares that "the Master is at hand" (see *Dracula*, pp. 151, 150). In the middle of the night, he even escapes and runs toward Carfax. In the days that follow, his behavior becomes even more erratic and violent.

Meanwhile, Mina writes to Lucy from Budapest, relating the details of her travel and reunion with Harker, whom she finds weak and troubled. The nun alludes to strange, horrible things but will not elaborate. Harker entrusts his notebook (where the "secret" of his madness is lodged; see *Dracula*, p. 156) to Mina, but she does not read it. They are married. Lucy sends congratulations and love in reply and announces that her own wedding is planned for September 28.

On August 24, when Lucy returns to Hillingham, her home in London, Lucy she begins a journal. Her strange dreams have continued since leaving Whitby, and Holmwood has noticed her decline in health. After "[a]nother bad night", Lucy speaks of a pain in her throat (see *Dracula*, p. 162). At the end of the month, Holmwood writes to Seward and asks him to come and visit Lucy. Seward visits the girl and diagnoses the cause of her condition as mental, though he notes that she is "somewhat bloodless" (see *Dracula*, p. 164). He tells Holmwood that he has written to Professor Van Helsing of Amsterdam, an "old friend and master . . . who knows as much about obscure diseases as any one in the world" (see *Dracula*, p. 165). Van Helsing comes to see Lucy and is concerned but offers no explanation. At first Lucy seems to improve, but then her situation worsens dramatically. Van Helsing and Seward undertake three separate transfusions in an effort to save her, taking blood from Holmwood, Seward, and Van Helsing. Throughout, Van Helsing's treatments are somewhat unorthodox and even baffling to Seward, including offering the ill girl garlands of garlic to wear around her neck as she sleeps. A few days of peace follow.

On the night of September 17, chaos seems to break loose. A wolf named Bersicker escapes from his cage at the Zooaulogical Gardens and returns half a day later, strangely chastened. Renfield breaks into Seward's office and attacks him with a dinner knife. Seward is injured slightly, and when the blood drips to the ground, Renfield falls to the floor and laps it up with his tongue, crying: "The blood is the life! The blood is the life!" (see *Dracula*, p. 201). Lucy goes to bed adorned with flowers as directed by Van Helsing but is awakened by a noise—like flapping—at her window. Soon her mother enters, concerned for her daughter, and lies with her upon the bed. A noise at the window is followed by a crash. When they see a wolf at the window, Mrs. Westenra clutches at the garlic, tearing it away from Lucy, and then dies of fright. Soon after, Lucy discovers the maids helplessly drugged with laudanum. She is too frightened to leave her mother. As specks begin to float and circle in the air before her, she writes farewell to Arthur and prays to God.

The following morning, Seward and Van Helsing find a horrifying situation at Hillingham: the maids drugged, Mrs. Westenra dead under a sheet, and Lucy pale and almost dead. They undertake another transfusion, this time using Morris, who has been sent as an emissary from Holmwood, as a volunteer. Even with this final transfusion, Lucy does not rally. Her griefstricken fiancé arrives. On September 20, just before she dies, Lucy asks Holmwood to kiss her, but he is stopped by Van Helsing, to the bafflement of the others. But Lucy thanks the professor for intervening, and then dies. Van Helsing ominously says, "It is only the beginning!" but will not explain further (see *Dracula*, p. 226). As they undertake funeral arrangements, Van Helsing continues his unorthodox behavior, searching through the family papers, placing a crucifix over the mouth of the dead girl, and tentatively suggesting a bizarre postmortem for the following morning. On this same day, Renfield once again turns violent, and the asylum personnel are forced to put him in a straitjacket.

After the funeral, Morris and Holmwood (who is now Lord Godalming, since his father has also died) leave for the latter's home. Van Helsing continues to speak enigmatically as he prepares to return to Amsterdam. Grieving, Seward concludes his diary and writes "finis" (see *Dracula*, p. 244). Meanwhile, on September 22, while Mina and Harker are in London, Harker is overwhelmed by the sight of "a tall, thin man, with a beaky nose and black moustache and pointed beard" watching a pretty girl outside an expensive jewelry shop (see *Dracula*, p. 238). He seems to suffer a relapse.

Beginning on September 25, the *Westminster Gazette* records an account entitled "A Hampstead Mystery" (see *Dracula*, p. 244). The story is circulating that young children have been straying from home late in the evening and, when found, claim to have been with a "bloofer lady". Some of the children are discovered with small wounds in their necks. An "Extra Special" edition of the *Gazette* follows, escalating the title of the story to "The Hampstead Horror", reporting the discovery of another injured child, left weak and emaciated (see *Dracula*, p. 246).

Meanwhile, although Harker seems to have recovered from his shock in London, Mina decides to read his foreign journal in hopes of better understanding his illness. She is left confused and frightened after reading it but is determined to be prepared for whatever comes, and sets down to transcribe the journal with her typewriter. On September 24, Van Helsing writes confidentially to Mina, introducing himself as a friend of Lucy and asking permission to visit, which she eagerly grants. He visits the following day, and Mina not only allows him to read her journal (recording the occurrences in Whitby) but gives him Harker's journal to read as well, begging him to help her husband. They all pledge friendship, and the Harkers promise to help in battling the Count. As Van Helsing leaves Exeter for London, he is horrified to see the headlines of the *Westminster Gazette*.

On September 26, Seward resumes his diary. Van Helsing returns from Exeter and claims that Lucy has been attacking the children in Hampstead. Seward is infuriated at the suggestion, but Van Helsing persuades him to come along with him, first visiting the latest child victim and then venturing into the churchyard in the early evening and opening Lucy's coffin, which, to Seward's perplexity, they discover empty. They wait through the night, until they witness a white figure approaching the tomb and retrieve another victim from the bushes nearby.

The following afternoon, Van Helsing and Seward return to the churchyard, reopen Lucy's coffin, and find her body, strangely beautiful and blooming. Van Helsing outlines his theory: she has been transformed into a vampire but without full culpability for her actions: "In trance she died, and in trance she is Un-Dead, too" (see *Dracula*, p. 274). He suggests that they call Morris and Godalming and then return to the tomb to cut off her head, fill her mouth with garlic, and drive a stake through her body (to free her from the undead existence).

The following day, Van Helsing persuades Seward, Morris, and Godalming to accompany him to the churchyard that night. They arrive late and find the coffin empty. They then wait outside after Van Helsing seals off the tomb with a putty mixed with consecrated Hosts. When Lucy appears with a whimpering child in her arms, they confront her. She first snarls angrily at them, then turns voluptuous and tries to seduce Godalming into her arms. Van Helsing wields a crucifix to repel her and herds her into the tomb. The men return home with the intention of returning the following day. At midday, the men return to the tomb and dispatch the undead Lucy—Godalming driving a stake through her body, and the doctors decapitating her and stuffing her mouth full of garlic.

After this, their plans for destroying Dracula begin in earnest. Van Helsing returns to Amsterdam for supplies and research, and the Harkers come and stay at the asylum with Seward (arriving on September 29). Although Seward is reluctant at first, Mina persuades him to allow her to listen to his phonograph recordings while he reads over her and Harker's diaries. After they have both finished, Mina and Seward reunite and marvel over what they have both learned. Mina persuades Seward to give her the last cylinder (which records what has occurred since September 7, when Godalming gave blood in the first transfusion) and to allow her to transcribe all of the phonographic recordings. She works late, transcribing newspaper clippings as well.

Meanwhile, Harker traces Dracula's boxes from Whitby to Carfax and collects papers to this effect. Then he assists Mina in arranging all of their combined information chronologically. On the night of September 30, they all meet for an official conference, in preparation for which Morris, Godalming, and finally Van Helsing read over the documented accounts collected and typed by Mina. Meanwhile, Seward, at Mina's request, reluctantly grants her a visit with Renfield. To Seward's astonishment,

Renfield is gracious to Mina and even prays a blessing upon her at their parting.

At their conference, Van Helsing delivers a lengthy lecture on vampires and on their foe particularly, including his history and his recent activities. Their conversation is interrupted by a gunshot, shattering a window. Morris informs them that he saw a bat at the window and went out to shoot at it. Van Helsing continues to outline their plan: to trace the boxes and "sterilise the earth" in them so that Dracula cannot "seek safety in it", then track down Dracula and kill him (see *Dracula*, p. 326). More immediately, he plans that Mina will remain and rest while the men visit Carfax. Before they leave for Carfax, however, Seward receives a message from Renfield. When the men go and visit him, the patient appears quite sane and begs to be released. After the strange visit with Renfield, which leaves the men thoughtful, they venture toward Carfax. Breaking in, they explore until discovering twenty-nine boxes in the estate's old chapel. They ward off an attack by rats. Upon their return home, they hear Renfield moaning, and Harker finds Mina looking oddly pale but sleeping softly.

On the morning of October 1, Renfield is sullen and uncoop-erative. Mina is troubled and overtired, which she attributes to disturbances in the night and strange dreams. Her health contin-ues to decline strangely. She visits with Renfield, who is kind to her. Further, the erratic behavior of the lunatic leads Seward to hypothesize that Renfield may have had contact with Dracula in the past. The men, during this time, continue their research: Harker locates six of the boxes on Chicksand Street, Mile End; six on Jamaica Lane, Bermondsey; and nine in a house in Piccadilly, recently purchased by "a foreign nobleman, Count de Ville" (see *Dracula*, p. 364).

Late in the night of October 2, Seward is startled by a loud cry from Renfield's room and by the report that Renfield has been discovered face down on the floor, covered with blood. When Seward and Van Helsing arrive, they find the patient with his back

broken and half of his body paralyzed. They immediately oper-
ate on his smashed skull, bringing some relief. Renfield awakens
and confesses his prior meetings with Dracula, who promised him
flies, rats, and moths. Later, neglected by Dracula and suspecting
that the Count had begun to prey upon Mina, Renfield attempted
to wrestle with him but was violently injured by the infuriated
Count. Upon hearing this revelation, Van Helsing and the others
rush away to the Harkers' room, where they find Harker trans-
fixed in a stupor on the bed by the window, Mina kneeling on
the bed, and the Count beside her, forcing her to drink blood
from a cut in his chest. Confronted by the men, who wield sacred
objects before them, Dracula disappears, leaving Mina hysteri-
cal and the men horrified and desolate. A quick exploration of
the house reveals that Dracula has destroyed all of their original
records, leaving only Mina's transcript locked in a safe. The attendant reports that Renfield is dead. Meanwhile, Mina provides an
account of Dracula's attack: the Count threatened Harker's life,
then, drinking blood from her throat, informed Mina that he has
preyed upon her several times. He then forced her to drink from
his chest.

Later in the day of October 3, the men decide to sterilize all of
the boxes, beginning at Carfax, then visiting each of the houses in
and around London. When Van Helsing attempts to purify and
strengthen Mina by placing a consecrated Host on her forehead,
it burns her, leaving a scar. Afterward, the men leave for London
and, arriving at the house in Piccadilly, break in and purify the
eight boxes they find there. Seward, Harker, and Van Helsing
remain there while Godalming and Morris visit other houses.
While waiting, they receive a telegram from Mina warning them
of Dracula's approach. Soon after, Godalming and Morris return,
reporting their successful sterilization of the other boxes. Dracula arrives, and the men confront him, but he escapes, swearing
vengeance. Returning to the asylum, the men stand guard over
Mina throughout the night.

The following morning, Mina suggests that Van Helsing hypnotize her to read Dracula's thoughts through her. From this, they deduce that Dracula is inside the final box and aboard a ship—judged by Van Helsing to be an attempt to return to the castle. After some investigation, Van Helsing is able to identify the most likely ship: *Czarina Catherine*, sailing from Doolittle's Wharf for Varna. While Dracula is at sea, they all feel an uncertain peace. Meanwhile, Van Helsing urges that they must continue to track Dracula down diligently; otherwise, he will spread his contagion. The men organize their plan of campaign and make preparations. They must depart from London on October 17 at the latest to reach Varna before Dracula.

The days pass, and they all wait, full of anticipation, for news of *Czarina Catherine*. Mina struggles visibly, insisting on traveling with them in pursuit of Dracula (as the safest and wisest course). A few days later, she asks the men to promise that, when she begins to change into a vampire, they will kill her and then dispatch her undead self. Then she asks Harker to read the Burial Service to her, deeply moving all listeners. Amid other travel preparations, Harker drafts his last will and testament.

They travel to Varna, arriving on October 15. Relying on their calculations and information granted through hypnosis sessions with Mina, they await the arrival of *Czarina Catherine* shortly and make preparations accordingly. After over a week of anxious waiting (October 24), Lloyd's of London, the insurer, alerts Godalming that *Czarina Catherine* has been reported from the Dardanelles. The days continue to pass, however. Mina becomes more lethargic, arousing Van Helsing's anxiety. Then, on October 28, Lloyd's alerts Godalming that the ship has bypassed Varna, entering Galatz.

Startled by this news, the men hurriedly rearrange their plans. Seward and Van Helsing share their increasing concerns that Dracula is using Mina to discover their intentions—a fear that seems to be confirmed by the fact that Van Helsing's attempts to hypnotize Mina are becoming less and less fruitful.

Meanwhile, the men hurriedly trace the events following the landing of *Czarina Catherine*. A man met the ship at the dock and accepted a box addressed to Count Dracula, then passed the box to a man named Petrof Skinsky. The men went to seek Skinsky but heard almost immediately that he had been found dead in a nearby churchyard.

While the men rest after their long day, Mina types up papers. From her notes, she concludes that she has made a clarifying discovery as to Dracula's plans: he is traveling by water, and most likely by way of the Sereth River. From this conclusion, they formulate new plans: Godalming and Harker will take a steam launch up the river to pursue Dracula, while Morris and Seward will take horses to follow along the river bank, and Van Helsing and Mina will travel inland toward the castle.

The action proceeds swiftly, with the three parties converging upon Dracula's castle. Harker and Godalming suffer a delay when the launch is damaged by their attempt to force their way up the rapids. As Van Helsing and Mina pass rapidly through the countryside, they witness the superstitious nervousness of the locals. Van Helsing's attempts at hypnotizing Mina become ever more unsuccessful, even as his anxiety for her intensifies.

On November 5, Van Helsing and Mina come within sight of the castle. After another failed attempt at hypnosis, Van Helsing encircles her with pieces of the sacred Host. Soon after, they are beset by the three women from Dracula's castle. He warns them off with a piece of the Host, and though they call to Mina, she is unable to move outside the circle. Leaving Mina sleeping in the circle, he ventures into the castle, finding his way down into the ruined chapel. There he discovers three "graves that are inhabit" and a lordly tomb inscribed with the name "DRACULA", which he sterilizes with a piece of the sacred Host (see *Dracula*, pp. 483, 484). He dispatches the three women vampires and returns to Mina.

The following day, Mina and Van Helsing witness the final battle against Dracula from a high rock. As the Szgany near the castle, they are overtaken by the four men. As a snowstorm flurries around them, and as the wolves gather, the men surround the gypsies, and a dramatic fight ensues. Morris is mortally injured, but he and Harker prize open Dracula's box and expose the Count. Harker slices the Count's throat just as Morris stabs through his heart. The body crumbles into dust and disappears. The gypsies flee, and Morris dies.

Seven years later, Harker writes a note. He and Mina have a son named after Morris. Earlier that year, the Harkers journeyed back to Transylvania to revisit the places where they suffered so much. Godalming and Seward are both happily married. They all meditate on the fact that almost all of their original documents are gone, but Van Helsing insists: "We want no proofs; we ask none to believe us!" (see *Dracula*, p. 496).

Words Made Flesh: Summary of Critical Appraisals and Study Questions

The questions posed in this section are not intended for examination purposes but are designed to prompt appropriate trains of thought for the student to ponder as he reads the work. Questions intended for examination purposes are to be found in the "Study Questions on the Text" at the end of the study guide.

Eleanor Bourg Nicholson: Introduction to *Dracula*

The success of *Dracula* is a baffling, not to say mysterious, business. From its publication, at which time it received mixed reviews, until the present era, when it has spawned innumerable spin-offs in film and fiction, the novel remains a conundrum. Investigation of the biographical and literary context of the novel will prove fruitful in seeking to understand this book and its mysterious tenacity, as will a study of the extraordinary and wide-ranging religious, legislative, economic, societal, and scientific influences endemic to the period. Beyond all of this, the heart of the novel is to be found in a dramatic tension between the ancient and the modern, a tension that is derived directly from attitudes established both at the time of the Protestant Reformation and more particularly during the period known as the Enlightenment.

The Enlightenment, in fact, proves to have been so comprehensively influential on the formation of the English Protestant Victorian understanding of life that it is an essential lens for the understanding of the appearance of vampirism in *Dracula*. The forebears of the Count do not turn out to be merely literary; he is part of a distinctive heritage of a vampire "epidemic" of the seventeenth and eighteenth centuries. This heritage is, in great part, derived from the established dynamic of religious tension between Catholicism and Protestantism, culminating in widely different understandings of the supernatural and the sacramental potency of objects. Indeed, it is these very questions—indirectly asked and perhaps never answered by the novel—that make *Dracula* the powerful novel that it is.

1. Briefly summarize the history of the vampiric "epidemic" outlined by Nicholson. What significance does this have for the development of the novel, in Nicholson's view? Do you agree with her interpretation?

2. What is the religious tension identified by Nicholson? Is she in agreement or disagreement with the account provided in Guilinger's essay ("Religion and Superstition in Bram Stoker's *Dracula*")? What is your opinion?

3. How does Nicholson explain the success and influence of the novel? Do you find this explanation satisfying and convincing?

Amanda Guilinger: "Religion and Superstition in Bram Stoker's *Dracula*"

Although scholarly attention to *Dracula* has increased significantly in recent years, interpretations have largely neglected the true significance of the novel, which is the supernatural struggle at its heart. The novel works within a very precise religious dialectic, built upon the idea that Stoker deliberately fashions Dracula as more than a mere monster—as a representation of the Devil and, even more important, as a direct inversion of Christ. Consideration of this, which must begin with the use of physical objects in the battle against Dracula, will at the same time illuminate the use of Catholic objects in particular, allowing us to consider the deeply important question: Does the novel evidence merely superstition, or is it demonstrative of a deeper religious awareness?

The novel is as rife with moments where its spiritual subtext is clearly shown as it is riddled with scriptural references. This is first and foremost developed, as noted above, in the character of Count Dracula himself. His language and his appearance, as well as his agenda for domination (setting up an alternative "eternal" kingdom to that of Heaven) and his means for achieving it (through a deliberate perversion of the sacraments), establish him as the inversion of Christ. His fellow characters are affected by this as well, especially the madman Renfield, who serves as an inverted John the Baptist figure. Even more important, the inversion of the Eucharist into the blood-drinking of vampires serves as a critical point of supernatural significance. This study does perhaps suggest a greater spiritual delicacy in Stoker, both as a novelist and as a man, than is often believed. Through all of this, an interpretive lens is provided for the novel that strikes at its dark and complicated heart.

1. Is there, according to Guilinger, a precedent for spiritual significance in Gothic literary tradition? Do you think it is an essential or an accidental element of the genre?

2. What theories does Guilinger put forward to explain Dracula's lack of reflection?

3. Explain the evidence of the "lack of anti-Catholicism" in Stoker's personal life. What effects of this can you see in the novel?

Jack Trotter: "The Cinematic Dracula: From *Nosferatu* to Bram Stoker's *Dracula*"

Dracula has fascinated filmmakers and filmgoers alike for nearly a century. Ironically, however, nearly all of the films that are *Dracula* inspired are completely unlike the novel. The universal trend has been to move away from the metaphysical significance of the novel to an emphasis on the humanity and physicality of the monster—a monster who has become a "postmodern tragic antihero". This trend began nearly two hundred years ago with the rise of the Romantic movement and its almost "vampiric" revolt against the "empiric" emphasis of the Enlightenment. The primary representative of this trend is Lord Byron, whose short story fragment was picked up by his friend and personal physician, John Polidori, and fashioned into "The Vampyre" (1819). The paradigm of the "darkly glamorous" Byronic vampire echoes down even into the modern day, tussling against the folklore paradigm (embraced by Stoker) that casts the vampire as supernaturally monstrous and bestial.

These two competing paradigms form the interpretative basis for a fruitful critical examination of film adaptations of the novel, seven of which are treated here. Murnau's expressionist masterpiece *Nosferatu* (1922), the magnificent first cinematic attempt at capturing the novel, provides an important counterpoint to and contrasts dramatically with the "drawing room melodrama" of Tod Browning's *Dracula* (1931). Terence Fisher's *Horror of Dracula* (1958) sets itself apart from preceding attempts by its ruthless and destructive modernization. Dan Curtis' *Dracula* (1973) works to make the monster sympathetic, while Philip Saville's *Count Dracula* (1977) carefully follows the novel's plot, though with a Byronic interpretation of the title villain. John Badham's *Dracula: A Love Story* (1979) is full of feminist posturing and little of the novel, while Francis Ford Coppola's *Bram Stoker's Dracula* (1992) both introduces a tortured romantic subplot and, in a "decidedly heretical fashion", reintroduces the long-dismissed metaphysical heart of the novel. These dramatically varied adaptations work together to provide a fascinating insight into the novel itself and the temptations and moral dangers that lie at its heart for even the most cautious of readers.

1. Describe the "archetypal Romantic vampire". What importance does Trotter attribute to the Byronic influence?

2. Have you seen any of the films mentioned by Trotter? Do you agree with his assessment of them?

3. From Trotter's analysis, what are the pitfalls into which adapting screenwriters, directors, and performers can readily fall in attempting to translate *Dracula* to the screen?

J. K. Van Dover: "Professor, Psychical Research Agent, Detective: Van Helsing's Role in *Dracula*"

Dracula is not merely an iconic piece of Gothic heritage. As early reviewers noted, it bears many similarities to another rising and important literary genre: that of the mystery novel. From its inception in the writings of Edgar Allan Poe until its heyday with the development of the Sherlock Holmes adventures by Arthur Conan Doyle, detective fiction grew to enjoy significant popularity and to follow a recognizable paradigm. *Dracula* works in fascinating counterpoint to this, borrowing from and yet not directly following this established paradigm. This is shown particularly in the character of Professor Van Helsing.

Van Helsing challenges the expectations of the admirers of Sherlock Holmes; he is a professional, contrasting against the enthusiast Holmes. Holmes, for all his bohemian displays, is a flat-footed empiricist; Van Helsing embraces both the scientific world (with his credentials) and the supernatural (with his sincere belief in the existence of vampires). Holmes uses a rational, scientific method to deal with mysteries; Van Helsing uses spiritually infused or supernaturally powerful tools. At the same time, the actions of Van Helsing provide as viable an exploration of the idea of detection as do those of Holmes. Nevertheless, in the end, the true central mystery (i.e., the vampire) remains unsolved, branding *Dracula* as an "un-detective" story.

1. Why does Van Dover suggest that the "community of lovers" is inadequate in battling Dracula? How does Van Dover's Beowulf analogy illuminate the reason he believes Van Helsing is a necessary addition?

2. Why, according to Van Dover, was it especially important for Stoker to establish Van Helsing's bona fides, contrasting with the amateur expertise of Holmes?

3. What statements are derived from the "incontrovertible conclusions" of Holmes' method? What statements are derived from those of Van Helsing?

Things to Think About While Reading the Book

The questions posed in this section are not intended for examination purposes but are designed to prompt appropriate trains of thought for the student to ponder as he reads the work. Questions intended for examination purposes are to be found in the "Study Questions on the Text" at the end of the study guide.

1. Be attentive to the contemporaneity of the story. Stoker's deep consciousness of the issues and prominent persons of the day is shown repeatedly through name dropping and through the particularity of the timeline. He chooses his setting with great particularity and detail (though not always with geographic or historical accuracy). How does this work in the context of a battle with a monster hundreds of years old? Does it give a greater sense of the immediacy of the threat? What is the place of time in the book overall? When is speed imperative, and how is this sense of urgency shown?

2. In addition to the pregnant timeliness of the story, pay careful attention to the form of the novel. Notice the varied types of records used and the interplay of various accounts of the same event. When are these varied types of records considered more compelling proof of the veracity of the account? When are the characters "metatextually" conscious themselves, making note of the fact that they are writing while they are writing? When are the various narrators unreliable, and why? When

are there inconsistencies or errors in the record, and should those be attributed to Stoker, as author, or the characters, as narrators? How much work do the various characters do to maintain the overall record? What effect does the overall structure have upon the experience of the reader? Is there a difference between the storytelling of someone like Dracula and the recording habits of the antivampiric league? Which characters do the most recording, and what effect does this have on the development of their personalities, especially in contrast to the others?

3. The influence of burgeoning modern scientific theories can be seen all over *Dracula*, and in varying degrees of legitimacy. The highly controversial claims of Darwinism, the emergence of new ideas gleaned through geology, and an increasing fascination with archaeology and other methods for investigating the ancient past all point to the supremacy of empirical knowledge. Popular pseudosciences, such as phrenology, hypnosis, and spiritualism, on the other hand, demonstrate the metaphysical confusion of modernizing man. Where does science empower the characters of the novel, and where does it bring confusion?

4. The novel is full to brimming with technological gadgets, including typewriters, phonographs, and even fledgling flashlights. How do the tools of modernity interact with the tools of antiquity? When are they useful, and when are they useless? Who wields them? How do they empower or handicap the progress of the heroes? To what degree does the form of the novel exemplify or deviate from the "scientific method"?

5. What is the relationship between enlightenment and faith in the novel? With science, technology, and medical advancement behind them, is there a place left for belief? What is the language of belief, and how does it play out across the course of the novel? Consideration of this point will be espe-

cially fruitful if examined in the historical and social context of *Dracula*. At the same time, do not forget to pay attention to moments when characters express belief or disbelief toward each other. When do they trust one another, when are they suspicious, and why? When are belief and trust appropriate, and when are they dangerous?

6. Similarly, consider the difference between superstition and belief (especially in the first portion of Harker's narrative) and madness and belief (especially in relation to the character of Renfield). The novel is as riddled with allusions to folklore as it is with complicated (and often confused) allusions to religion. What is the difference between science and folklore? What is the difference between science and religion? Who is most representative of each? Contrast the folklorish theories of vampirism with the use of Roman Catholic sacramentals. (When you consider science in this light, be particularly careful not to ignore the representatives of pseudoscientific practices.)

7. At the end of the Victorian period, the notion of the virtuous woman serving as the "angel in the house" was being challenged by notions of the rising "new woman". Think about this and consider the centrality of women to the novel—their virtue and innocence as paramount to the sustenance of the society, and the devastating effect of their victimization. Are these characters developed, and if so, how? What are Dracula's attitudes toward women in general? What are the attitudes of the men toward the women, and of the women toward themselves?

8. The professional association and aptitude of the characters is often referenced or utilized in the novel. What proves to be of greater value: the accreditation of the expert or the enthusiasm of the amateur? What are the roles played by law, medicine, and scholarship? What actions result from research, and what actions are spontaneous? Is there a difference in Dracula's approach to research and that of the antivampiric league?

9. The theater played an important part in Stoker's life. Consider both the ways in which his Irish heritage influenced his sense of the theatrical, and the ways in which his friendship and professional collaboration influenced the development of *Dracula*. This will be shown primarily in the most atmospheric and violent moments in the novel but should be seen in many of the drawing room scenes as well.

10. Count Dracula has captured the imagination of readers and moviemakers for decades—but who is he *really*? Stoker's creation might be called a vampire in mosaic form; what are the attributes of the vampire as Stoker presents him? What influences can be discerned therein? How does Dracula's character develop? How does he present himself to his fellow characters? How does he affect his victims? Note that he is predominantly absent; be attentive to the manner in which he comports himself when he is present and how he is described when he is absent. Notice as well the differing accounts given concerning him and attitudes expressed about him—is he enduringly evil, or is he at all a sympathetic figure? (Be careful to see Stoker's vampire as Stoker actually created him, not as a filmmaker might want to perceive him. At the same time, recognize what might motivate a filmmaker to portray him differently.)

Study Questions on the Text of *Dracula*

Part One—Knowledge of the Text

1. What is the significance of the date on which Jonathan Harker travels to Castle Dracula?

2. How many servants are employed in Castle Dracula?

3. Who is Harker's employer, and what is his fate?

4. What is the occupation of Wilhelmina Murray?

5. What is Dr. John Seward's diagnosis of Renfield?

6. What types of pets does Renfield adopt, and in what order?

7. How does Dracula travel to England, and where does he first arrive?

8. How many boxes does Dracula ship to England?

9. What is the pseudonym used by Dracula to purchase the house in Piccadilly?

10. What is the name of the Godalming estate, and what relationship does Arthur Holmwood have to it?

11. What sort of procedure does Van Helsing undertake for Lucy in her illness, and how many times does he do it?

12. What is the name of the wolf that escapes from the London Zoo, and what is the significance of that name?

13. Which of the main characters falls victim to Dracula and is turned into a vampire, and what is Van Helsing's solution to "kill" the young undead?

14. What happens to the original Dracula records (letters, newspaper clippings, journal entries, etc.) transcribed by Mina?

15. How many homes does Dracula own in England, and where are they located?

Part Two—Essay Questions

1. How are the fates of Lucy Westenra and Mina Harker similar, and how and why are they dissimilar? What do these women, and all of the female characters of *Dracula*, represent in the novel and in the context of Victorian England?

2. What does the literary form of the novel contribute to the development of characters or the overarching plot?

3. What role do science, medicine, folklore, and religion play in *Dracula*, and to what degree do they entail moral culpability? (Contrast particularly the professional authority of Dr. Seward and Professor Van Helsing with their occasional manipulation of legal detail or haphazard usage of scientific tools or sacred objects.)

4. What is the difference between madness and faith? How does the character of Renfield stand up to this question? Does he develop, both as a character and as a moral agent, and if so, how?

5. Van Helsing declares, "We have on our side power of combination—a power denied to the vampire kind". What does this mean? What is the difference between the vampiric hordes and the community of men and women battling against Dracula?

6. "The blood is the life!" cries Renfield. With the asylum patient's remark in mind, what is the significance of blood in the novel?

7. The members of the antivampiric league at times inadvertently enable Dracula to fulfill his designs—usually through mistakes or ignorance. Are there moments when they are morally culpable for what happens? What parallel (if any) can be drawn with the degrees of culpability implicit in the behavior of vampires or other Dracula victims?

8. How successful a power is Dracula really? Why isn't Transylvania overrun with vampires, and why does he fail in his attack on England?

9. Sherlock Holmes memorably castigated the idea of vampires as "pure lunacy". Even Van Helsing acknowledges repeatedly that the notion of Dracula defies the belief of "enlightened" man. Is the novel "pure lunacy", or is it honestly frightening? If the latter, how does it function as a frightening book?

10. Is the novel's ending satisfying? Why or why not?

Notes

Notes

---*Notes*---

Notes

Answer Key for *Dracula*

Note to Teachers: This answer key can be removed
before the study guide is given to the student.

STUDY QUESTIONS

Part One—Knowledge of the Text

1. He travels on the eve of Saint George's Day (the Feast of Saint George), on the midnight of which "all the evil things in the world . . . have full sway" (see *Dracula*, p. 20).

2. None; Harker comes to suspect that Dracula oversees all of the housekeeping on his own.

3. Harker works for Mr. Peter Hawkins of Exeter, who dies suddenly midnovel.

4. She is an assistant schoolmistress before her marriage.

5. He calls him "an undeveloped homicidal maniac" and later clarifies this further by dubbing him a "zoöphagous (life-eating) maniac" (see *Dracula*, pp. 110, 111).

6. He catches flies, then spiders (to which he feeds the flies), then sparrows (to which he feeds the spiders, and which he eats raw). He begs to own a kitten.

7. He travels first by leiter-wagon and then by ship, landing on the English coast at Whitby.

8. Fifty

9. Count de Ville

10. The estate is called Ring. Holmwood is the only son and heir of Lord Godalming, and when his father dies, he assumes the title and becomes full owner of the estate in his own right.

11. He performs a blood transfusion, which he does four times.

12. Bersicker; the Berserkers were Viking and Norse warriors who wore animal skins into battle and so terrified their opponents by their frenzy and ferocity that they were sometimes believed to be transformed into beasts—a possible source for many werewolf legends as they arose in popular folklore.

13. Lucy becomes a vampire, and to "kill" her, Van Helsing proposes to drive a stake through her heart, fill her mouth with garlic, and cut off her head.

14. Dracula burns all of the papers and destroys the cylinders on which Seward recorded his journal entries. A copy of Mina's transcription is locked in a safe and is consequently spared destruction.

15. There are four houses: one in Essex, just outside London (Carfax at Purfleet), and three in London itself (the house at 197 Chicksand Street, Mile End; the house at Jamaica Lane, Bermondsey; and the house at 347 Piccadilly).

Part Two—Essay Questions

1. *How are the fates of Lucy Westenra and Mina Harker similar, and how and why are they dissimilar? What do these women, and all of the female characters of* Dracula, *represent in the novel and in the context of Victorian England?*

The writer of this essay should demonstrate an understanding of the situation of women during this period, especially with the tensions between the ideal of the "angel in the house" and the rising notion of the "New Woman" (upon which Mina herself wryly comments; see *Dracula*, p. 136, 137). Beyond this, there is a wide scope for exploring the ways in which women are a central and vital point for social growth—and thus a target for societal destruction. This is shown most vividly in the novel's conclusion, where Mina's redemption and fertility signal the return to social normalcy and health. Thus, the most obvious relation between Dracula and the mention of Jack the Ripper in the author's preface is of course to be found in the Count's deliberate seeking out of female victims. This is not merely a sexual issue; it has deep social connotations. When the women are attacked, it is a comprehensive blow against the men who love them and who should defend them. The repeated pledges of enduring friendship sworn by men to Lucy and to Mina will prove important here, especially since both of these women fall prey to the vampire. Mention may also be made of the three women in Dracula's castle, to the innkeeper's wife in Bistritz, and to many other secondary female characters.

2. *What does the literary form of the novel contribute to the development of characters or the overarching plot?*

   While this question should not be seen merely as an invitation to demonize or deify Stoker's talents as a novelist, an essay can either do battle with or endorse the commonly held opinion that the novel is full of poorly developed characters. Are the characters superficial or realistic, and are they developed in spite of or because of the form of the novel? The writer should show at least a passing familiarity with the heritage of the literary form, particularly with regard to the epistolary form. An understanding of the Gothic and mystery traditions could also prove very valuable. Does the form of the novel contribute to its suspense, and if so, when and how? Are the writers of the various documents better developed than characters who do not write? What of Dracula himself? The writer should make use of the critical essays without simply recycling their content and should try to see beyond the stylistic to its larger effect on character and plot.

3. *What role do science, medicine, folklore, and religion play in Dracula, and to what degree do they entail moral culpability? (Contrast particularly the professional authority of Dr. Seward and Professor Van Helsing with their occasional manipulation of legal detail or haphazard usage of scientific tools or sacred objects.)*

There are many examples to be explored here: Dr. Seward and Professor Van Helsing are perhaps the two most scientifically and academically qualified characters in the novel. For Van Helsing especially, his academic credentials make him an almost unstoppable force in the novel. At the same time, this essay topic may inspire a closer look at scientific theories and the ways in which they are used to support hypotheses and provide justification for potentially immoral actions: e.g., Seward diagnosing Renfield as an "an undeveloped homicidal maniac" and then drugging him so he can study his illness, or Van Helsing diagnosing Lucy as a "young . . . Un-Dead" and then manipulating sacred objects to trap and destroy her (see *Dracula*, pp. 110, 277). Even more compellingly, this essay might address the lonely, deserted death of Renfield. Is there ever a moment where the behavior of the antivampiric league is truly unjustifiable or inexcusable? Is there ever a moment where their actions might even bear a comparison with the ruthless activities of Dracula himself?

4. *What is the difference between madness and faith? How does the character of Renfield stand up to this question? Does he develop, both as a character and as a moral agent, and if so, how?*

Renfield, one of the most fascinating and bizarre characters in *Dracula*, is perhaps the most surprising to readers—a nonvampire with fanatical vampiric appetites. The writer of this essay should take note of the moments when Renfield seems to be a victim, not only of Dracula, but even of Seward as well. His brief relationship with Mina must also be taken into account. Larger questions are encompassed in the consideration of his character: What is the significance of his overwhelming lust for lives and attendant terror of souls? How does he embody the various kinds of imprisonment presented in the novel: imprisonment of the body, of the mind, and of the soul? Is there a distinct correlation between sanity and belief (cf. 1 Corinthians 1:25)?

5. *Van Helsing declares, "We have on our side power of combination—a power denied to the vampire kind" (see* Dracula, *p. 321). What does this mean? What is the difference between the vampiric hordes and the community of men and women battling against Dracula?*

This essay topic opens up larger questions of family and society, juxtaposed against a necessary analysis of the Count's ambitions. The trajectory of the novel flows clearly from thoughts of marriage to the fruit of marriage, represented by the Harkers' son. At the same time, there are many social circumstances to keep in mind, including the effects of urban development upon the nuclear family. While the critical essays do not address this point directly, the contextualizing understanding provided therein should prove helpful in writing this essay. The writer may even identify important moral analogies to the threat posed by vampires, particularly with regard to the perversion of sexual and marital normalcy.

6. *"The blood is the life!" cries Renfield (see* Dracula, *p. 201). With the asylum patient's remark in mind, what is the significance of blood in the novel?*

This essay can approach the topic of blood from a myriad of vantage points: blood as a life-giving bodily fluid; blood as representative of ancestry; blood as a path to redemption (i.e., redemption through violence, which shatters the boundaries of physical reality); blood as a category of race; blood as a symbol of violence; and Eucharistic Blood, poured triumphant from the Cross. All of these, and more, are discernible threads in *Dracula*. It is indeed a novel gorged with blood. Is this why the story is frightening or disturbing to many readers? Some of the most horrifying moments in the novel are the most bloody; why is this?

7. *The members of the antivampiric league at times inadvertently enable Dracula to fulfill his designs—usually through mistakes or ignorance. Are there moments when they are morally culpable for what happens? What parallel (if any) can be drawn with the degrees of culpability implicit in the behavior of vampires or other Dracula victims?*

This is not an irresponsible question; it is one that may readily present itself to the minds of readers. How many times is Lucy Westenra left alone, exposed as a victim to Dracula's bloodlust? How many times is Mina Harker likewise left alone by the men who have already seen the fate of an undefended young woman? Even more horrifyingly, when Van Helsing and Seward flee to the Harkers' bedroom and discover the carnage left by the Count, why do they not feel a single qualm at leaving Renfield to die alone in his cell, a broken creature in a pool of blood? (There is another possible approach to the question: some overzealous critics have put forth the theory that Quincey Morris works deliberately in cahoots with Dracula, noting the number of times that Morris' actions or inaction seem to assist Dracula in a concrete way. This theory is not entirely unacceptable if it is well supported and if it is approached with a ludic enthusiasm rather than with motives of postmodernist revisionism.)

8. *How successful a power is Dracula really? Why isn't Transylvania overrun with vampires, and why does he fail in his attack on England?*

This is a partly facetious line of questioning, but it is an important point to be considered and should provoke a thoughtful and even entertaining essay. The evil powers of Dracula are manifold; Van Helsing outlines them repeatedly and at length, and the results of his villainy are clearly shown in the fates of Lucy Westenra and Renfield, not to mention all of the unnamed victims he leaves in his wake. Nevertheless, the fact that he fails—and fails repeatedly—must be acknowledged. Is this simply demonstrative of a moral tipping of the dualistic scale—the representatives of good must triumph over the physical personification of evil—or is there something more at play? Perhaps the writer of this essay should reconsider Dracula's intent more carefully: Is he really bent on world domination, or is his goal simply the destruction of individual souls? The latter involves a far more personal attack, which must therefore be all the more terrifying. Depending on the essay writer's approach, he should probably account for the "look of peace" on Dracula's face as he dies (see *Dracula*, p. 492).

9. *Sherlock Holmes memorably castigated the idea of vampires as "pure lunacy". Even Van Helsing acknowledges repeatedly that the notion of Dracula defies the belief of "enlightened" man (see* Dracula, *p. 424). Is the novel "pure lunacy", or is it honestly frightening? If the latter, how does it function as a frightening book?*

For this essay, the novel's ties with the Gothic and horror tradition might be considered. Is a Gothic novel something that the enlightened man must look down on? Is there value in something that is simply enjoyable—even if it is "pure lunacy"? This may lead to the consideration of the question whether *Dracula* should really be considered a classic novel. Further, the entire notion of enlightenment could be explored. Is the opinion of the "enlightened" man to be relied upon where a novel about vampires is concerned? Knowledge of Victorian attitudes toward what was appropriate reading material and what was not (especially where refined young ladies were concerned) may be helpful here. There is even a metatextual note that could be struck: the characters themselves read their own account of their adventures and register varying degrees of horror. When is the novel frightening to its characters, and when is it frightening to its readers? Why?

10. *Is the novel's ending satisfying? Why or why not?*

This question can draw upon the themes addressed in a number of the questions above: the form of the novel, the development of its characters, and the theatrical elements that are or are not employed by the author to introduce suspense. *Dracula* is a truly innovative book in many ways. Is it a disaster, or is it a masterpiece? The introduction and the critical essays all tend toward the latter interpretation and can guide this essay. At the same time (as the writer of this essay should be aware), the novel was ignored by literary critics for the greater portion of its history. Why is this? This essay question is fashioned to invite the expression of the writer's personal opinion and experience—a valuable starting point for critical analysis, if properly wielded.